LEO
A Baby Lion's Story

Executive Producers, John Christianson and Ron Berry
Illustrator, Lara Gurin
Art Director and Book Designer, Eugene Epstein
Writer and Creative Director, Kathleen Duey
DVD Mastering and Editor, Stephanie Carlson
DVD Soundtrack and Song Composed and Produced by George Fogelman
DVD Audio Mixed and Mastered by Robert Cartwright and George Fogelman
DVD Video Narrator, Daniel Krasner
DVD Song, Sung by Ian Brininstool and George Fogelman
DVD Video Footage, the British Broadcasting Company
Production Manager, Doug Boggs

Distributed by Ideals Publications
A Guideposts Company
535 Metroplex Drive, Ste 250, Nashville, TN 37211

ISBN 9780824918170
Printed and bound in China

MY ANIMAL FAMILY®

LEO

A Baby Lion's Story

*I*t was a hot day on the Serengeti plains and the air
shimmered with sun and heat. Almost all the grown-up
lions had climbed into the trees to nap. They would sleep
until evening. My sister tried to climb the tree. She couldn't.
My brother and I tried. We weren't quite strong enough yet.

My mother just watched until we all gave up. "Stay close to me," she told us in her deep, rumbling voice. Then she led us toward the river. She knew a place where we could all cool off.

We walked beside my mother for a long time,
but when my sister spotted a fallen acacia tree,
we all ran toward it. Our mother followed us.

The branches were wide and it wasn't too steep. Mother didn't mind waiting for us. She knew we had to practice climbing. We have to learn how to do everything the grown-up lions can do.

We all raced to make it to the highest branch. My sister got there first, but we were right behind her. I was really excited. Then I slipped and I almost fell!

My mother roared—not a loud roar, a soft one. "Hang on," she was saying, "you can do it." I dug my claws into the bark and pulled myself back up. Then we all held very still and looked out over the land.

From the branch, we could see all the way to the river!
There were elephants splashing in the cool water
and antelope were grazing on the riverbank.

My mother roared again—and this time it was a very loud roar. Three lionesses answered her from far away, somewhere near the river. That meant most of the mother lions were already there. It was time to go.

*I*t was a long, hot walk to the river.

We all waded straight into the water and took a long drink.

Then my brother and my sister lay down to nap.

My mother was the first one to go to sleep! The shade

was wonderful. The sound of the river was soft and sweet.

But I just wasn't sleepy. I kept wading in the shallows,

listening to the birds.

Suddenly, I noticed an odd sound I had never heard before coming from behind a big sickle bush. I lowered my body like my mother does when she is hunting.
I crept forward very slowly, crawling through the leaves.
It was a little bird, whirring its wings, drinking flower nectar.

*T*hen I heard another sound.

Breathing?   I looked up.

There was a giraffe staring down at me!

It looked as tall as a tree.

Crouching, I waited until

the giraffe walked away, swaying

like grass in a soft wind.

I wished my mother was with me.

I was never scared when she was close by.

I knew it was time to go back.

But then I saw a lizard.

It saw me too, and it ran!

I had to chase it!

I ran as fast as I could, but the lizard skittered through the grass so fast I couldn't keep up. I made one last, long leap. . . but it got away.

When I stared at the grass and trees in front of me, they didn't look any different from the grass and trees behind me. I turned in a slow circle.

I was lost.

At first, I thought it would be easy to find my mother. But it wasn't. I could smell the river, but I couldn't tell which direction the scent was coming from in the still air. I wasn't sure what to do, I just knew I needed to get back to my family. The sun would go down before long.

When I saw the tree with the low, wide limbs,
I ran toward it. I jumped as high as I could and dug
my claws into the bark. Then I worked my way upward.
I knew I had to make it. And I did!

$\mathcal{F}$rom the high branch, I could see the river.

I could see my family. My mother wasn't sleeping now.

She was pacing the riverbank. I knew what she was doing.

It was getting late and she was looking for me.

When I got down,

I knew exactly which way to go.

*T*he giraffes just watched me run past this time. I found the sickle bush and went through the branches. Then I was on the path by the river and I ran even faster.

My mother was very happy to see me. I sat still while she licked my face and smoothed my fur. That night, I snuggled close to my brother and sister. It was wonderful to be back with my family.

The **My Animal Family** project
was created by a team of people
who care about children, their own and yours.
We all want to help kids learn about themselves,
their families, and their world.

The Illustrated Book

Our picture books are written with care and beautifully illustrated.
Every story is about the realistic adventures of a baby wild animal,
an accurate portrayal shaped by current behavioral research.
Each story gives parents and grandparents opportunities to talk to
their children about life, home, and family.

The Activity Website

The *My Animal Family* creative team includes game and website designers, too. We have built a **safe**, fun place for kids to play "animal" activities online. At **MAFKidsClub.com**, children will find their favorite animal friends in their native habitats. Set in arctic snow, tropical forests, oceans and deserts, the games help pre-readers get ready for school and keep beginning readers happy and busy. Games are leveled so that each visitor can build confidence and master basic skills. The creative team has worked hard to make the website friendly, fun, interesting and safe for your kids.

The Live-Action Animal DVD

Every book includes a live-action DVD that features **award-winning BBC** wildlife video footage. Carefully edited for young children, the footage gives them a glimpse into the reality of each baby animal's life. Kids learn about the cooperation that helps animal families survive and thrive, and about the habitats they live in.

LEO
A Baby Lion's Story

Leo goes exploring, then has to find his way back to his family

KOROW
A Baby Chimpanzee's Story

Korow learns to climb high enough to pick her own fruit.

ELLA
A Baby Elephant's Story

Ella helps protect a newborn baby elephant in danger.

NANUQ
A Baby Polar Bear's Story

Nanuq saves his bossy brother from a foolish mistake.

MY ANIMAL FAMILY®

Welcome to the Club!

My Animal Family is a new kind of children's club. With books to read, DVDs to enjoy, games to play, puzzles to solve and adventures to share, it's the kind of club every child dreams of... *"where the fun and good times never stop."*

Membership begins with the purchase of a beautifully illustrated storybook. Every story in the series is captivating and stars a baby animal in a realistic, family adventure... animal families that include elephants, lions, chimpanzees, polar bears, and many more...

Use the secret passcode on your membership card to explore *www.MAFKidsClub.com* There are no advertisements or fees